Sam was at lunch.
He had an egg salad
sandwich — again.

"Pete, I'll trade sandwiches with you!" Sam said.

"All right!" said Pete.

So Sam and Pete swapped
sandwiches.

Sam looked at Pete's
sandwich. It was soggy.

"Joan, I'll trade sandwiches
with you!" Sam said.
"Okay!" said Joan.

So Sam and Joan
swapped sandwiches.
    Sam looked at Joan's
sandwich. There were
pickle slices in it.

"I'll trade sandwiches with anybody!" Sam shouted.

6

All the other kids had
finished eating.

Now, Sam wished he could have his own lunch back. Dad made the best sandwiches.